BROKEN EGGS

PETER PEGNALL

PUBLISHED BY
LAPWING PUBLICATIONS
c/o DENNIS & RENE GREIG
1 BALLYSILLAN DRIVE
BELFAST BT14 8HQ

PRINTED BY

TEXTFLOW SERVICES
SCIENCE LIBRARY
LENNOXVALE
MALONE ROAD, BELFAST
TEL: 663591

ISBN 1 898472 23 8
LAPWING POETRY PAMPHLET
PETER PEGNALL
PUBLISHED 1995
COPYRIGHT REMAINS WITH AUTHOR

Lapwing Publications gratefully acknowledge the financial assistance of the Arts Council of Northern Ireland and The UK Foundation for Sport and the Arts in the publication of this pamphlet.

'WITH GRATITUDE
TO DENNIS AND RENE
TO NICK, GRAHAM, MARTIN AND PETER
ALL OF WHOM HAVE HAD CONSIDERABLE EDITORIAL
INFLUENCE.

THANKS ALSO
TO JANE,
THE LONG SUFFERING AMANUENSIS.

CONTENTS

BEHIND THE LINES	7
BORN AGAIN	8
BRENT EXPLAINS...	9
BROKEN EGGS	10
DAVE'S DAD	11
DEAR JOHN	12
DISINHERITANCE	13
LONELY, LIKE NORMAN	15
FLATMATES	16
FUCK THIS FOR A LARK	17
STARDUST	17
RYAN	18
FRED ASTAIRE	18
HUNTED	19
GOING NORTH	20
IN PLACE OF PRAYER	21
IN THE PINK...	21
IN THE RED	22
THROUGH THE ROCK	23
INTERROGATING THE SILENCE	24
ITS ONLY MAKE BELIEVE: FOR BECKETT	25
JUMP. DON'T JUMP	26
MEDEA	27
ON THE FENCE	28
GETTING AWAY	29
ONE IN THE EYE	29
OPHELIA IN THE LIVING ROOM	30
PERFORMANCE	31
A POSTCARD FROM PORTUGAL	31
REMEMBRANCE DAY	32
GENERATIONS	33
SILENT MOVIES	34
STILL	35
STREET CLEANING	36
WEST PIER ROMANCE	37
THE LAST ACT	38
JUDY TALK	39
EPIPHANY	40
BRIGHT GLANCE	41
BEGINNING	41
HICCUP	42

*for my family
and in memory of my father*

BEHIND THE LINES

This year they lost their leaves in springtime;
a great whoosh and the horse chestnuts spindled
like old fingers. A squashed sun drowned itself.

You might hold your body like a flower,
scared of crushing, glad to be close to colour,
making plans hour by frightened hour.

It would only be snatched if you made it -
there are burglars in each conversation
if you live like a saint you've betrayed it
making plans on the beach for a nation.

There isn't much of a family,
John Major. If you're 'sick and tired'
of bolstering no-hopers why not think
'one day I might be a no-hoper myself.'
Who knows?
                From ten Downing Street to night shelter?

Would your old friends cluster round?
does your one O-level keep you warm?

When O when will your clichés hit the ground?

BORN AGAIN

He wanted it all. Another penis,
beside his tongue. And still he'd hanker
for more warm passages, sighs of welcome...
however drunk, there'd be arms to fold him,
legs to grip. He must have known how adored:
one of the gods slipped away for a lifetime.

But a lifetime was far too long. I laughed
as he sank: Francis playing his wild self,
gulping pills like smarties, picking fights he'd lost,
going too far for my frightened sake. Not so.
He plunged faster, deeper than I'd ever glimpse,
'no way out' printed across his pretty face.

You might catch him now in the shopping precinct;
tubby, bald as the guru he apes by rote,
dishing out pink and purple booklets,
grinning like a toad in treacle,
 rattling a tambourine. Come back, little boy.
Flowers grow in dung. Live fits, snug as death.

BRENT EXPLAINS, APOLOGISES, AND FINDS GOD AT LAST

Leah, Leah, why didn't you raise your voice?
I know I can be quite inconsistent. I know
I should have known it was that slag Janice;
can't you see it's because I love you? Why
couldn't you cry out, louder? I know
you'd never, never, how could I think it?

You're still the little girl on the swing. Up
down, up, down. 'Push me higher higher!' you'd shriek.
I'd stand back and follow your legs flying,
waving, like swallows, like scissors, open,
shut. No more Sunday mornings in the park.

You were my first, foolish thing, Leah, my own
and not my own. I'd strained so hard for your
love. Someone scratched a moustache on your face,
scrawled a prick between your thighs, between your lips
I took a chisel to it. My own, not
my own. Smirched. Plundered. A gush of deep red.

Forgive me, Leah, that last violation,
those probing fingers: always a virgin.
Always.
       I should never have doubted you.
I can see Janice now, unfolding latex
on some ebony staff; taking it in.

If ever I've needed an angel it's now.

BROKEN EGGS
(for Kit Wright)

Blake was mad. Clare was mad. Plath was mad. I'm
O.K. at the moment. I don't think crows
slouch like scavenging border guards. That God's
abandoned the game. That, stripped of reason,
we see. If only you'd glimpsed those poor sods
rocking themselves to some dark place who knows
where, dribble gunging their lips, stiff with crime
and refusal, you'd know what fucking treason
spills from intellectuals, hungry to hang
like limpets on those quaking souls who sang
without hope.

And me, too. I'll pound my rhetoric
grimace to order, take my squashed place
in the hall of mirrors, out on the edge ...

The fact is that when your mind flops off track
you might get free enough to fall apart.

And no blazing ladders into the clouds,
no field mice scarcely twitching the long grass,
no small bright wound can put you together,
put you together, put you together
again.

DAVE'S DAD

Dave's dad played gypsy violin:
kebabs by candlelight, love songs
squealing in a Soho cafe;
long, black hair flopped in greaselets,
his giant nose danced through the smoke.

He'd gabble crazed philosophy,
sucking tea from a grubby mug;
we'd share cigarettes and despair
in a small front room in Shepherd's Bush,
stinking of damp and dope and cat's flux.

The young girls he chased all escaped,
like his wife years before. Dave stayed,
long enough to find the first one
who'd say yes. His dad sank slowly,
clutching a book of Zen and a plastic rose.

DEAR JOHN

Keats had trouble with women. The filthy
pieces wrapped his fingers around his nail,
pumped his clack, the water spurted warm;
They were to blame, he stifled in their feathers.

Fanny irritated him, danced with soldiers,
taunted his solitude. Once he drenched his pants
and once he hid in her room. She knew, un-
dressed slowly. Keats learnt the word 'succulent'.

So Byron may have got it wrong; Keats right;
not an article, but love killed him:
'I eternally see her figure
eternally vanishing.' But why?
He was no Victorian. He was no
Byron, abused, incestuous, self-loathing.

Well - the last! I suppose they all,
we all; hiding; images for escape,
for confinement. And the women? You can't
tell me they don't enjoy tormenting.
Even that lesbian couple in the Thai restaurant,
gazing under their skins, even they knew
I watched, chewing my squid deliberately.
They sat in the window, a little theatre;
what chance does a young man have with that?

On with the sweetmeats, the cordials, John:
if you can't beat them - beat them - beat yourself

DISINHERITANCE

The streets of Hounslow sparkle in winter,
frosty grey slabs, patterns to skip across.
Nowhere to live, really, bricked with small fears,
acceptance. Go shopping when you can't stay in.

Fat women, fatter men, ugly children
snivelling. Teenagers slouch like empty coats.
The pubs are stuffed with refugees at home,
telling short stories, as far as they go.

I could ride my bike across stubbled fields,
I could scrump apples with my friend Timmy,
I could take root in the park, girl-gazing.
A real boy, snot-sticky, alone at night.

And that's what I can't reach. Did I tremble
or shriek? Or was I warm when light faded
and were the voices downstairs promises
they'd keep? What are dreams worth in Hounslow?

You're not Winston Churchill, you're not a girl,
you're not a weary detective. Peter.
Peter, like a pixie with a bad eye,
Peter, hug him tight, poor little Peter.

I hate you. You never come when I call,
you're always getting me wrong. Stop laughing.
I love the girl on the train, her white socks,
her neat hair. She loves me too, I can tell.

The thing is, can you live? Accumulate
experience like coins, it tumbles, slides,
slips away. The world's no theatre, but act,
you're on, you were then, behind the curtain.

It's hard to describe who you are. A child
says 'me' like an object, trying to hold on.
And a voice still happens to you, like breath
you don't intend, can only hear at night.

I want that little boy, he's hiding now
like he did with Fiona under the bed
kissing and kissing. I think he despised
her, couldn't face his friends or family.

And is that it? Saying 'no, I didn't,
you've got the wrong man, I was just passing
and feeling that way. None of it's true now.'

If you believe your story, tell me how.

LONELY, LIKE NORMAN

Norman led with his nose. His long nosed dog
snouted home most nights, Norman parabolating
in the freezing air behind. Six pints,
a game of arrows, the same glum badinage
day in day out. It's a comfort, boredom,
until you almost can't tell what you'd choose
from what's chosen. Pay up and play the game.

But one day his small face, led by his nose,
pressed close to mine. He lived with his old dad,
who discovered a dirty mag under his bed.
Where else?
He shredded it and fed it to the fire,
the small fire they could afford. Norman,
I may say, was a simpleton, an allowed
cretin. So it didn't matter when leggy girls
giggled and flirted. He has a sweet face,
Norman, but his nose gets in the way a bit.
There's no harm in that little hard on.

Anyway, no more magazines. But he dreams,
does Norman, he told me so, close and quiet,
he dreams a goddess in platform heels,
in stockings and suspenders, in black lace.

When he wakes up, there's no bugger there.
But himself.

His dog leads him the only journey he knows.

Soon you'll be gone. When I wake up there'll be
no bugger there. No wonder I hate trains and boats,
no wonder I see time like a sliver of light,
there and not there at all. Like Norman, I'll live
when no one else could believe how or why?

Like Norman, I'll learn to let go
the only fantasy I'll ever feel
in that squirled up softness under the sheets
in that place that no one allows me to be.

Unless you whisper close when I'm not looking.

FLATMATES

I'm down here punishing my typewriter:
one more article for Gardeners' Monthly,
'Hardly Hedgerows: Fir-Trees in the Suburbs'.
It's November and the sky's yellow,
the city shrivels, there's no promise
in the air. This ancient machine
marches like a bailiff through my poverty.

Upstairs I can't hear a couple making love,
Can't guess their sly caresses, whispered lies,
don't imagine they hear me on the job,
how they pity me. Listen in as I pace and sigh.

Perhaps I'll move. Buy an Amstrad.
Swap my square of concrete for a square of green.

Somewhere outside the window. Somewhere clean.

FUCK THIS FOR A LARK

I'm a scarecrow. You don't scare, ignore
my snazzy rags, my outstretched arms. You feed
at will, bounce across the land. I see you soar
and scribble vicious signs over my head.

I cannot crane to see you, cannot read,
cannot do nothing. Rooted here, fruitless,
little children mock and fear me. I'd bleed
now if I could, whine: 'it's me. Can't you guess?'

Just imagine when you're tucked up at night
when shrieking winds and bone-soaking fogs assault
the bare copses, the brown earth, when owls bite
into velvet bodies, when all the bloat

creatures that guzzle and grow in your veins
are rampant and smirking: just imagine
me dumping my cross, nose pressed to your pane.
Just imagine creeping downstairs: letting me in.

STARDUST

She lingers by the rain spattered window,
Gazing blankly into a bright city:
Inside, fusty hallways, voices fading
Behind closed doors, her own, echoing room.
Almost afraid to move, she lifts the phone
And lets the purr dangle from her hand;
The plastic clunks back on plastic. No one.
Babbling TVs the shipping forecast,
A child's exhausted whimper, gushing pipes.
Her eyes glint for a few special seconds -
A gulp of gin, a palmful of capsules:
She joins Marilyn in the noiseless night.

RYAN
("I wish I'd stayed in bed" - Michael Ryan, Hungerford)

It might have been red-hot blue videos,
Remote control flicking from crisp-white sheets,
Soon to be crusted; or maybe pigeons,
Those mangy crappers. delighting
The solitary eye. What about darts?
No contact required, no questions to duck.

It had to be guns, credit card killers,
Licensed to play about a bit. Picture
Yourself, larger than life, remarkable
As lightening, bored with the music of death,
Cornered by the shame you've always suffered;
Imagine no forgiveness, forever.

FRED ASTAIRE

Describing arcs and circles in the air,
Black snakes around a Malacca cane; your face
Like a silly skill, your voice thin, tremulous,
you glide amongst triangles of white tulle,
Effortless perfection, draining every
Current of yourself. Like playing the fool,
Like composing a soufflé, you capture
Happy victims. Sidewalks, subways, trash cans
Painted glorious colours by your feet .....
Even bed-sitting rooms dance in the corner -
Farewell arthritis! So long varicose veins!
A star flickers, who cares about the screenplay?

Why did they display you near death, a weak
Broken dolly, scarcely able to speak?

HUNTED

I'm on the run. You wouldn't know it. Watch
my eyes, they're watching yours. In Sainsbury's
I act normal. Pile biscuits on bog roll,
nudge my trolley into your legs, fumble
for pen and cheque book. I sign my real name:
clever eh? For five years, invisibly,
MI5 have been closing in. They wait,
like cats in the long grass; my TV feeds them
everything they require, it dreams me.
I've written fifteen letters to Thatcher,
incognito. I'd be at my wits' end
if I wasn't so smart, one jump ahead,
that's me. My brown polyester trousers
merge nicely. I'm too busy for a job;
anyway you can't sit still in this game.
Forget everything I've told you. It's more
than my life's worth; I'd rather you ignored me.

GOING NORTH

Friday, five fifty-five: Waitrose, Woodley.
Tins and icy polythene bulging fat
from the trolleys. Highland water crushes
my chocolate bananas. I've forgotten
the muesli biscuits, soon I'll move next door
for Bulgarian Sauvignon, Spanish
Ribena. But for now, my arm aches, my mind
whimpers 'Why? Why? You've done your time this week:
First Form Drama, Fourth Form Self-discovery,
Sixth Form weeping for the world. Coffee breaks
with my colleagues! Surely even Sam Smiles ....'

This degrading reverie is broken by -
       "Sixty five thousand, third of an acre,
       old Yorkshire stone. Thirty minutes from Leeds,
       twenty to York. You can really breathe there -
       asthma's a thing of the past. The locals
       accept you when they know you're there to stay.
       Lashed out on a crumbling chateau in France:
       water, electricity, all you need."

Her woolly leggings, her relentless drone,
my ecstatic relief I live alone.

       "The kids? Love it! Hardly ever see them!"

IN PLACE OF PRAYER

It's always too early. Thomas and Martha,
drowned at play in the Severn's wide waters,
they held tight and lugged each other down.
Leaving the world, they changed it, they remain;
not all the seas swallow one moment's grief.

But call them by name, those unformed faces;
like small fingernails piercing our palms they grip,
they plunge us deeper than memory, we choke
on borrowed words. Death separates the living;
each new funeral rehearses the last.

Jamie smashed through a shop window, bled white
as his motorbike throbbed. Fourteen years old -
too young by far, too old to be an angel;
stopped dead; a church filled with children's voices,
his young sister's face set in silent rage.

I lack ceremony. How shall I let go?
This year one more 'accident'. A girl, Robyn,
crumpled like a paper doll. The next world
mocks this one. O pray for the living
make shapes we can see in the gathering dark.

IN THE PINK; NUDE BATHING AT BRIGHTON

A librarian, he shelves his week-day
self and gets his clobber off. Dangle, strut,
picking his way along the pebbles. Tubes
and flat cushions of flesh sprout along the shoreline.
Be naked and free! If only he'd come
before; this might have been the life he's missed:
forty-five; bald; a mouth you'd never kiss.

IN THE RED

As a child they locked me in a cupboard;
Screaming as they thrust me inside, I screamed
At the closed door. My bleeding fingers scraped
Furrows in the knotty pine, my eyes stung.
My brain spiralled into a black chasm,
Dizzy, frantic, feeble unbelieving.

Later, when sudden light drank the darkness
I cowered away from their open arms,
Hugging my knees, rocking to an fro,
Tunnelling into my twisted tummy:
"I wasn't a good boy now, I wasn't!"

Late springtime, after a long fever,
I wandered in Nana's unkempt garden;
Fighting through an arch of eglantyne,
Bubbling my skin with deep red,
I found my funny face in a drop of dew
And tasted lilac in the living air.

The "middle one": troublesome, conniving,
Whinging, coercing my way to power,
Never enough. It seemed that in my dreams
Scarlet regiments bore down upon me,
Tongues of fire stung horrible confessions
From my trembling lips: waking veiled my eyes.

"Caroline's got a slot, not a winkie!"
Or so they said I'd said some lost teatime -
Two brothers, no sisters must have sweetened
Those early forays into no man's land.
As far as I know I left it at that.

But in the covered hammock,
Peter and Patricia, two five year olds
Crushed each other breathless for hours on end.
A space-ship, an island, an ocean liner,
A little chunk of heaven in Hounslow!
Her blonde curls, her blush, her spotted knickers
Under folded legs in school assembly!

Reader, I married my memories
long before I knew what was going on.

THROUGH THE ROCK

Your love clings like candy-floss on my lips;
I'm on the ghost-train, alone, in winter.

I can see you on Sunday afternoon,
frightened. Cleaning the car like a disease.

I'm sweet and brittle. The greeting runs through
my stick of rock: fuck you for having me.

INTERROGATING THE SILENCE

I hate poems. What was that you said? Print blurs the
issue.
                If you can't connect with your fingers,
if you stand apart when the landscape's painting
folds and shadows in motion. if you can't even touch
when it's heaven here -
      (Tiny white smiles
                      dying in the blue
              trees hunched like beggars uphill
     only the wind for rebuke or response)
You might as well admit the enemy;
you might come clean under the white spotlight.

But never, never write a poem when
you choke; when you paraphrase excuses -
is it exorcism or orgy?

Have you noticed how people speak quickly
when they're afraid or lying? Do they ask
themselves why they wallpaper the silence
with repeated patterns
of a reshaped past?

I'd like to get out of the noise and sit
where goldfish forget the last circuit
and babies are born in the warm wet undergrowth
and heaven extends like a borrowed blanket.

IT'S ONLY MAKE BELIEVE: FOR BECKETT

A long, thin garden path. I raced like mad
up and down, up and down, fat cheeks aflame.
I could never lose, never really win.
'Look at that child, gasping. Call that a game?'

I did my best to belong, shape up,
I could never understand, couldn't see
what it was they wanted, what they believed;
my voice complied, became the other me.

So, books and school plays, weaving classroom lies -
glamour tinged with acid. Smirking sometimes,
my friends came back for more. I found a place
improvising scorn, cloaked in easy rhymes.

One day the walls fell down, my bubbles blew
in a cold wind. I had nothing to wear
but invisible costumes. A pale sky
circled a skulking figure who wasn't there.

Along came Beckett - Molloy, Malone, Krapp -
gasbags punctured by their own perceptions,
solo turns in an abandoned theatre.
I learnt to trust solitude, the last deception.

As he went on, he narrowed down so near
your bones felt unfleshed. Terrified, I read
like an addict, rehearsed the laughter
his words first inspired. Now this: 'Beckett's dead.'

JUMP. DON'T JUMP

It's a house without windows. As if, running
through glue or shifting pebbles you sag and there's
nowhere else to go but trudge trudge so bravely
so aimlessly. And then, moments before you wake
from corridors of puzzled faces a glimpse -
clear sky and an open heart and soaring wings;
the weight clams down and you may as well not move
and you move through lead or woollen clouds pressing
closer than your own breath.
          You may as well march like a circus clown,
head held high for the next laugh. Or in my case,
a walk up and down, lamenting the pain
people don't, apparently, begin to feel,
their hurrying greedy unsatisfied eyes -
I'm sure they'd be grateful for my concern;
for these scornful unbelieving prayers -
like a stone mason, I carve my own face
in living gargoyles, become who I see.
          Harder than this, someone loves you and touches
soft where you like and her gaze speaks softer
and her love's the only language you know
and you can't answer even though you hear quite clearly
And it breaks her heart and it breaks your heart
and you button up for another long swim,
as if you could fool either or you,
as if the song of self-hatred rang
like a glitter of new minted coins
or a baby's first cry in cradling arms.
          And then there's the craggy coastline where Edgar
clutched his father's life although the surge sucked
him downward, although he knew it was all up;
and it was all up, but for gratitude -
"You loved me after all. The world is possible."

MEDEA

There is a window. There are faces.
There is panic. This, I am told, keeps people
going. There is no information. We
might be queuing for the Dachau train;
we might be anxious to board. There are women
acting as if their lives depended on it.
There are men affecting insouciance.

I do not think we are to be trusted.

Inside (once inside the fever lulls)
          a great hollow, cherubs in stucco,
red velvet, coats strewn on folding seats
ice cream at a price, a murmur, polite rage:
"I'm sorry (for the second time) I'm so sorry."
"It doesn't matter." Gritted teeth. Thin smiles.

And below. Much below, the half-lit space,
a few russet leaves in a small square pool;
great brazen panels closing in.
Our noises chuntering into silence
and a kind of wind, a kind of animal,
a kind of haunting; voices not volces.

She is regal, Medea, her agony
towers. At times I'm looping over the edge,
plunge to my death - don't do it - she
doesn't do it. She is Diana Rigg
she goes home and eats cheese sandwiches, she
does not smile yet. she is Medea. I
know why she hurts so much, I've been left flat.
I should like some of her courage. 'Medea
is not mad. Medea is not mad.' Fuck -
ing hell. Can we really do these things? Did
Jason fall so far? Did he sink home gladly
as if it were all in the game?

I do not think we are to be trusted;
we have been trusted with a terrible thing,
we have failed or failed to see our failure
often and often. Those women would do
I don't know what for those tickets. We men
are weak, duplicitous, easily fooled.

And there is no catharsis; mouths open
like clams; susurrations; alphabets; ohs!

ON THE FENCE

His face red with indignation and booze,
The politician mimics platitudes,
Revealing nothing. And I'm forced to choose
Between bloated fascists and trendy pseuds
As if the answer lay in knowing answers -
A barn dance caller yelling at the dancers!

"But surely something must be said?" Daily
We hear of some new outrage: war, famine,
Caterwauling lies as the ship gaily
Steams towards the iceberg. The price of sin
Is always paid by the innocent,
Always us. "I'm sure you see what I meant".

Apocalypse looms, almost fascination
For toy soldiers and badge - bedecked club members -
The fatal blast "a total vindication." -
"We told you so!" intoning from the embers.
"Where do _you_ stand?" Confused, appalled, ashamed:
And now I've said so really can't be blamed.

GETTING AWAY

A year after his illness. They've bought
the station buffet at Lewes, surprise
travellers with Earl Grey Tea, spinach quiche,
pottage du jour. Mozart tinkles on tape,
she chats breezily, arranges dried flowers,
half-certain that he's safe in the kitchen.

ONE IN THE EYE

Stationed by the piano, my pink plastic
eye patch the centre of the room, I sang.

'Rudolph the red-nosed reindeer
Had a very shiny nose.'

I opened my throat like a baby bird
and let fly. My family wept. My star glowed.

Four years later, in the grey Hillman Minx,
I became Elvis in 'Love me Tender'.

Laughter. I wavered on, a corncrake
in lark's feathers. 'Put a sock in it do,

Peter. 'In the rear-view mirror I looked O.K.
Eye not too wonky, quiff brylcream rigid,

my lip quivered. But I'd learnt already
that you mustn't cry when it really hurts.

OPHELIA IN THE LIVING ROOM

It's a rich and sickening story. She died
making no sense out of it, dressing up
to go under. Much too easy for us,
picturing despair, sharing what went wrong,
turning away as if that were enough -
slipped free. She simply couldn't face it,
gathered flowers like a little girl, clutched
the cold air, sang snatches of old songs, cracked
the world in a still green looking glass. Men
blame themselves, strike attitudes.

Our lives continue, headaches, small worries
closing in like china dogs. Tragedy
happens elsewhere, under blood-red skies,
in books, rooms we'll never quite enter. No.
This is it, nothing more special to come;
you scream and I babble half-excuses,
numb with disbelief. What did you expect?
Clichés fit close, like goose pimpled skin.

And, yes, the girl defined herself in death;
misused by her Daddy and her lover,
all three remembered that way. As she strolled
towards the water, did she feel each step,
know exactly where she was going?

I'd like to think there's something I've missed. Some
lost intangible that love promises
and death can scarcely be said to provide.

PERFORMANCE

Why do you do this? Piranha faces
Poised for the slashing laugh, the lethal yawn:
Dark images of inadequacy,
Acid imprints of imagined scorn.

Expectation thrills the foyer. Voices,
Staccato sharp, clamour and resonate.
Backstage it's chatter or silence, the same
Snake pit inside; these last minutes you hate -

But step out and let fly, your parachute
A tattered rag, yourself, the searchlights rake
The chill sky above a terrified town -
And still you sing, and still the house comes down.

A POSTCARD FROM PORTUGAL

A man standing by a bill board
At the edge of the road.
Dust, sand, stones, dry grass,
Sun already sizzling the broken tarmac:
A labourer, waiting to be carted to work,
He's been there for an hour at least.

Fuck me, it must be tiring.

REMEMBRANCE DAY

It's cold, this evening. Somewhere frost, even snow.
Beating retreat from the school play, a bearded man
explains, slowly, how a victory
when so many died was no victory.
His daughter seems reassured by his words.
There are lovely wars tonight. Bosnia
again. And I guess there's something brewing
under the peace shutters in Ulster. Whizz bangs
and burning crosses last week in Lewes.
      And so on and so forth.
            What takes my breath
is a row of fourteen year olds in Khaki,
unbearded faces bristling for attack.
Their wooden red guns don't fool me. They'd shoot
to kill. They'd do anything they're told. They'd die
like their great grandfather's brothers died;
like snowflakes, like poppies unfrocked, wind-blown.

GENERATIONS

My grandmother waited for years. At last,
one winter's evening, she let go. Her eyes,
milky blue, forgot to remember. Now
I forget and tell myself stories of love,
last words, sad little tableaux that cling tight
like the child I imagine in her arms.

She must have made love once. Cased in her nightie,
'rested' in Hind head after confinement,
torn inside. One child more than enough,
she settled for collapse. Those long afternoons:
tea, spying the neighbours, more tea, T.V.
they'd have happened whatever stars she'd seen.

And still she got dressed to go out. Dressed up.
Powder clogged in the wrinkles. Hat and scarf
poised for attack. Slippers in the High Street?
Oh dear me no. Some things you don't let slide.
But she hated each day like a sentence
she'd never serve. Nothing was all right.

So she punished her daughter, who punished
her by giving more and more, complaining
like she was the nicest, hardest done-by
creature in history. Guilt and duty,
household gods crowding the mantelpiece,
years at a glance swallowed in pretence and fear.

They were all afraid. They'd lived through World Wars,
buried babies, woken ten thousand times
in the same room. If I'd known the unknown
I'd have choked on my tea and biscuit, screamed
until they smothered me. Now it's too late.
Just make it up as you go along.

SILENT MOVIES

My next door neighbour's gutter's dripping, splat
splat splat. On the yellow washing line,
a row of, a necklace of raindrops. They
catch the light and I think of Andrew Marvell
as I peer close, hoping to see more.
The back yards, the rooftops, the red leaves
how many paintings won't I paint this autumn?
How many moments skim across like
a riderless scooter, like a Martian on a quick trip
to the blue planet. To the place where they all
run like Buster Keaton in Big Trouble,
their eyes brimming with panic and self-pity.

This is where I live, but I long for elsewhere;
oh, not the quick dive downwards, nor some evening
in Siena, not really. Call it a stillness,
a place too private to wrap in words,
but only words can get you there, maybe.

I'll do almost anything to avoid
reflection. A friend, a sixty year old woman
glimpses a witch in shop windows. Bad enough,
but, what if you catch your mind unawares?
Won't you spin and spin like Rumplestiltskin,
or as usual, will nothing happen and
you'll still be around, scratching the earth
for something to do. And something to do
with that. As my hippy pals used to say
PAY ATTENTION. You can hear the grass grow.
It made sense as long as you didn't ask why?

STILL

There are quiet corners, even in chaos;
the other day, stifling through, at the point of'
or 'nearly had a nervous breakdown') somewhere
a voice, or a glance; enough to let go,
a few moments where it doesn't matter.

You can get that with friends, when they sound as if
you're clever or funny enough to have friends
like them. And you drink as if you're thirsty
and gesticulate somewhat. But that's not it,
that's dancing for the camera, that empties.

What it is doesn't have a flavour,
or a line. There's no painting or poem,
no moss-green gate back into childhood.
A monk might get there, looking at the wall;
it seems like gliding, as if the soul
really were wings across a timeless sky.

So don't try for it. I'm talking to you,
Peter, you'd worry yourself to shreds
in a sacred garden, you'd squeeze nature
like a famished lover. Let your certain
knowledge of how small you are, how forgettable
ease your way slightly. You can't choose what lasts.

STREET CLEANING

He took his own life. He's taken anything,
he's taken us for a ride, he'd taken
liberties. Now he's taken away the last
time ..... He was here, he was crazed, abusive,
we had to think of the others. Now think -
that crooked dark shape in the doorway. Think.
Always think. Think of the others. Think he's
dead so once he was alive, once a pink
pudgy shape on someone's lap. Squalling. Son.
Brother. Words of consolation. Ice picks.

Think of the others. Ask why it's warmer
in the morgue than on the streets of England.
Ask the ghost of William Blake if we've built
Jerusalem; ask Satan if he's glad
the pavements in Knightsbridge glister with gold
the hearts in Knightsbridge platinum hard. Ask
God if, perhaps, he's a family man.

He is dead. I was told his name. His face
as they slung him out of the drop-in club
I didn't see. It was yellow when they found
him; a sort of grey-yellow fringed with filth.
Nobody's fault.
          There is a spectre of happiness
in this wretched place. It plays us like toys,
wound up toys with painted smiles. It sends us
to desert play-pits with coke in our nostrils,
avocado oil in our nooks and crannies.
We need the break. We come back and tell our friends.
I'm surprised they know who we are, so relaxed,
so changed in some deep, cosmetic way.

If only that man in the doorway glimpsed
some other world. Perhaps he did. Perhaps
he does.

WEST PIER ROMANCE

Tonight the West Pier floated into the sea
glowing like a Christmas tree in Norway;
some of us danced for the first and last time
reckless and graceful. The moon smiled, the stars
singled out shy lovers risking fingers,
folding like velvet. Saxophones gargled
nostalgia, it was Scott Fitzgerald, it
was a Monet in your auntie's attic.

There's a pink grapefruit on the horizon,
it's five-thirty and cars are ironed out
along the coast road. The pier's crumbling fast,
but you can dream can't you? Like a sad captain
skimming his wheel chair past the winos
and the silent bandstand, I remember
things that never happened. Waltzing in the wind.

THE LAST ACT

Each day like starting again. Like inventing
movement and speech. After tumbling from dream
to dream, all forgotten, the room's a box,
the staircase somewhere to climb down. I read,
swallow words crawling like ordered insects
across numbered sheets. Every now and then
something catches in my throat, my stomach,
as if Zola's black and white images
coloured my own pain. What pain's that? Not much.
Dispossession. The life that can't believe.
Forty years flattened to a cardboard shape -
or a stunted tree clawing at the wind;

my body's unpeeled but I'm still alive.

Imagine. Take control. Speak the possible
and fix a scene to fill the empty space:
your hand in his hair. His tongue in your mouth.
My voice on the telephone as you touch .....

Again: to walk pavements we'd wandered,
knowing, insisting that you're dead. Elsewhere.
The sickness coagulates, nourishes.

Go on. This may be precisely the point
it's like a photograph of agony;
changeless, futile, the statement of itself.

However far you fall, there's further down.

JUDY TALK

My brother's really stupid.
Well, he's quite cool actually
but he's got this in-tell-ect-ual girlfriend.
She doesn't approve. Doesn't approve of
skirts. Pink. McDonald's. Football 'cept for girls' football.
Girls. Ladies. Big cars. My mum. My dad. Money.
Nuclear Reactors. Silly photographs.
Me and my pet rat. My brother most ot the time
'cept she stays over and drinks mum's whisky
or dad's gin. She doesn't like my nighties,
even the old one I suck. She talks to the T.V.
tells it off lots. Which I think she's bonkers
but leastways she's leaving me alone.
My friend Spike put Billy in her bed.
Billy's <u>his</u> rat. She cried for hours and pinched Spike,
but I say only babies go to bed day-time.
She bosses Mike lots and bosses me lots
she bosses me to be more bossy
I'm bossy enough Spike says Spike's right
we always go where I want Spike likes it
Spike's my friend, Mike's my brother, he's stupid
but not so stupid he won't dump Her when I tell
I'm not telling you what I'll tell, it's bad, guy.
She'll be out of here super-sonic
then he'll go back to Cathy and I'll borrow her lipstick
'n climb on her shoulders and watch East Enders
and tell her secrets 'n give her chewing gum
'D'you want some?'

EPIPHANY

You know those white geometries in de Chirico?
as if there were no human life, only light, shadow,
angle after angle of stone brilliance;
it might be better, sometimes, unpeopled.

All the more rigid our shapes, then, statues,
fixed glares, like virgins surprised by one of the gods
like madmen facing the chasm of their being.
After all, I suppose I belong in flesh and blood,
favour those raunchy, sweating Brueghel beanfeasts,
bellies, codpieces, grins wider than watermelons,
pigs carving themselves at the round table.

But it's tempting, the clean lines of absence,
the lost town framed in its last microsecond;
like Pompeii, like the Grecian urn,
like this morning above the mossy orange rooftops of
Silves
where the dazzle slices here and there and there.

The only sound the frenzied racket of small birds;
and only me to see, only me to listen
only me to blab the secret in my airy tomb,
as if the album of forty years were white paper,
                    smudged, crumpled, but white,
annihilating.

BRIGHT GLANCE

Already in bed, I'll shut my eyes,
nearly. Don't miss a curve, a triangle,
however fast you shed those small, white things;
it's the sweetest show in town, every night.

As if this weren't enough, when we tumble
or clutch like lovers in a marble frieze,
locked in until the morning, I'll replay
how you bend, unclip, fold away, arch upwards.

Twice over. And twice again. Here you are,
closer than thought, a breathing miracle:
'this is no dream', although delight dreams itself:
image and act soar like dancers, like flame.

BEGINNING

I loved you long before. You were the child
marching out of the mirror, making faces
when the world wasn't watching, if you smiled
I climbed inside, warm in secret places.

Where did you go? I looked for you everywhere,
by the lake in winter, by the sea
when the wind whipped my eyes, rain raked my hair
fell into other arms. Found only me.

Between now and then, you slowly appeared
or I slowly noticed that hollow ache,
echoing all I'd longed for, all I'd feared:
Re-learning to love, preparing to break.

HICCUP
(a translation of 'Hoquet' by Léon Damas)

AND
    I'd pointlessly gulped seven mouthfuls of water
    three or four times in twenty four hours
    back comes my childhood
    in a hiccup gasping out
    my instinct
    like a cop scragging a thug

    disaster
    talk to me about disaster
    talk to me about

    My mother was in requirement of a son with
                        beautiful table manners

    Hands on the table
    the bread is not for cutting
    the bread breaks itself
    the bread is not to squander
    the Bread of the Lord
    the bread of the sweat on your father's brow
    the bread of the bread

    A bone is for eating with constraint and discretion
    a stomach must be polite
    and each polite stomach suppresses its belch
    a form is not a tooth-pick
    do not, not blow your nose
    in the sight
    in the light of the Whole World
    besides, you must sit bolt upright
    a well educated nose
    does not mop clean the plate

And besides and besides
and besides in the name of the Father
                            of the Son
                                of the Holy-Ghost
at the end of each meal
        And besides and besides
        and besides disaster
talk to me about disaster
talk to me about

My mother was in requirement of a son who'd
                swallowed the book of etiquette

        if your history lesson has not been
                          memorised
        you will not go to mass on Sunday
        shining in your Sunday Best

        This child will bring shame on our name
        This child will become our name in the name
                                        of God

Shut your mouth
Have I told you or have I not told you that you must
                                      speak French
the french of France
the french of the french
french french

Disaster
talk to me about disaster
talk to me about

My mother was in requirement of a son
the son of his mother

'You didn't talk nicely to our neighbour
yet again your shoes are filthy
you're for it if I catch you in the street
or on the grass or the Savane
under the shade of the war memorial
mucking about
bashing up so and so
little so and so who wasn't even baptised!

Disaster
talk to me about disaster
talk to me about

My mother was in requirement of a son so very do
so very re
so very mi
so very fa
so very sol
so very la
so very si
so very do
re-me-fa
sol-la-si
      do
It's come to my notice
that yet again you did not attend
your vi-o-lin lesson
a banjo!
Oh no and again no, sir
you must learn that our kind of person does not
                                      abide
neither ban
nor jo
neither gui
nor tar

Mulattos don't simply don't do that sort of thing
leave that to the wogs.